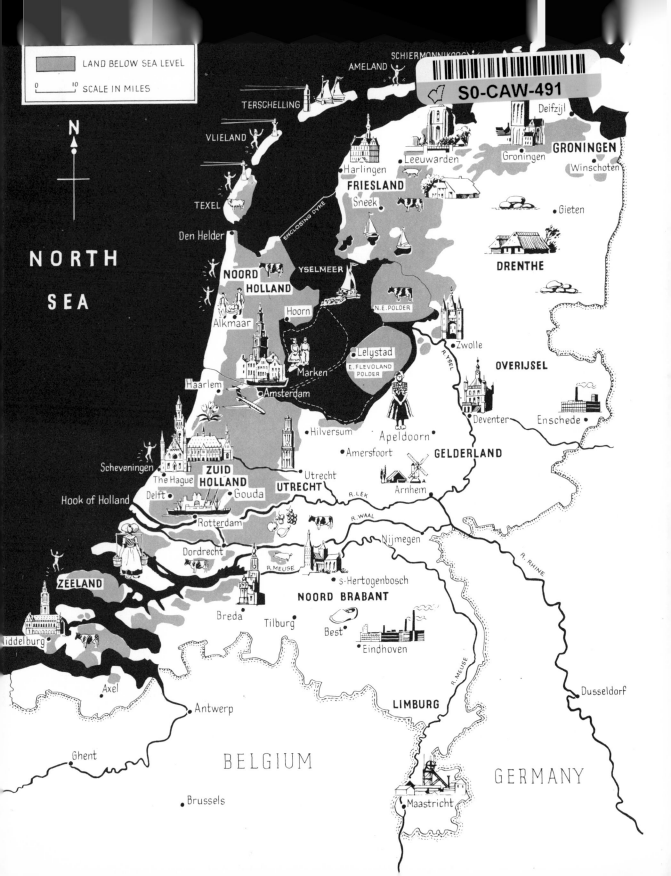

LAND BELOW SEA LEVEL

0   10   SCALE IN MILES

N

NORTH

SEA

SCHIERMONNIKOOG

AMELAND

TERSCHELLING

VLIELAND

Harlingen

Leeuwarden

Deifzijl

Groningen

GRONINGEN

Winschoten

FRIESLAND

Sneek

Gieten

TEXEL

Den Helder

DRENTHE

NOORD

HOLLAND

YSELMEER

Hoorn

N.E. POLDER

Zwolle

Alkmaar

OVERIJSEL

Lelystad

Marken

E. FLEVOLAND
POLDER

R. YSEL

Haarlem

Deventer

Enschede

Amsterdam

Hilversum

Apeldoorn

Amersfoort

GELDERLAND

Scheveningen

Utrecht

Arnhem

ZUID
HOLLAND

UTRECHT

The Hague

Delft

Gouda

R. LEK

Hook of Holland

R. WAAL

Rotterdam

Nijmegen

R. RHINE

Dordrecht

ZEELAND

R. MEUSE

s-Hertogenbosch

NOORD BRABANT

Middelburg

Breda

Tilburg

Best

Eindhoven

LIMBURG

Axel

Dusseldorf

Antwerp

Ghent

BELGIUM

R. MEUSE

GERMANY

Brussels

Maastricht

ENCLOSING DYKE

Looking at HOLLAND

Looking at

ANNA LOMAN

Adam and Charles Black London
J. B. Lippincott Company Philadelphia and New York

Volendam

HOLLAND

Looking at Other Countries

Looking at HOLLAND **Looking at JAPAN**
Looking at ITALY **Looking at SPAIN**
Looking at GREECE **Looking at FRANCE**
Looking at NORWAY **Looking at ISRAEL**
Looking at DENMARK **Looking at SWEDEN**

Further titles in preparation

Grateful acknowledgement is made to the following
for their permission to reproduce photographs :

Fotografie Steef Zoetmulder NFK 32b
David Gadsby 37b, 39b, 40c, 54a
Doeser Fotos 25a
Gemeente Amsterdam 20a, 21a, 32a, 32a, 33
Keystone Press Ltd 46
KLM Aerocarto NV 6, 28
Nationaal Fotopersbureau 21b
Netherlands Postal & Telecommunications Services 20c
Persfotodienst 8
Philips Ltd 41a
Royal Netherlands Embassy 12, 14b, 16, 17a and c, 24,
29, 40b, 41b, 49, 52b, 57a
L. van Leer & Co NV 7, 10a and b, 11a and b, 13, 14, 15a
and b, 18, 19, 20b, 22, 23a and b, 26a and b, 27, 30a and
b, 31a and b, 34, 35, 36, 37a, 38, 39a, 40a, 42, 43a and b,
44a and b, 47, 50, 51, 53, 54, 55, 56, 57b, 58a, b and c,
59, 60
VVV Amsterdam 21c, 45
VVV Leeuwarden 17b, 48b
VVV Rotterdam 25b
The illustrations on pages 62 and 63 are reproduced from
prints published by the Pallas Gallery, London
The photographs on the book jacket are reproduced by
permission of L. van Leer & Co NV

The maps are by H. Johns

Efforts have been made to trace and acknowledge all
copyright holders but full acknowledgement of any rights
not included here will be made in subsequent editions

ISBN 0 7136 0131 0

FIRST EDITION 1966, SECOND EDITION 1967, REPRINTED 1969, 1971
© 1967 **A & C BLACK LTD 4, 5 & 6 SOHO SQUARE LONDON W1V 6AD**
LIBRARY OF CONGRESS CATALOG CARD NO: 66-10905
PRINTED IN HOLLAND BY **L. VAN LEER AND CO NV AMSTERDAM**
AND REPRINTED IN GREAT BRITAIN BY **JARROLD & SONS LTD, NORWICH**

CONTENTS

The Country

Seen from the air the country of Holland looks like an enormous jig-saw puzzle. The entire surface is cut up by innumerable canals. These drain the land and very often they lie *above* the level of the surrounding countryside.

Holland is the name by which the *Kingdom of the Netherlands* is usually known, especially to people of other countries. In fact the name only applies to the two western provinces, Noord and Zuid Holland. The other provinces are: Groningen, Friesland, Drenthe, Overijsel, Utrecht, Gelderland, Zeeland, Noord Brabant and Limburg. The name *Noord Brabant* reminds us that Holland and Belgium were once united: the Belgian province of *Brabant* lies immediately to the south. On the east, the country is bordered by Germany, on the north and west by the North Sea.

The eastern and southern parts of the country are fairly high, but the western provinces are very flat and low, as they have been formed by the mouths of four rivers—the Rhine, the Waal (a branch of the Rhine), the Meuse, and the Scheldt. These rivers flow into the North Sea, one of Holland's oldest enemies. Nature has given the country a fine protection against this enemy in the form of a wide belt of sand-dunes along the coast, but in spite of this the low-lying parts need constant care and supervision.

In the past the sea has often rushed in with terrible effect. In several places you can still see where the coast-line has been broken. In order to strengthen the sand-dunes the Dutch, always fighters against the water, have planted a tough, coarse grass called *helm*, which prevents the sand from being blown away by gales.

Where the sand-dunes are insufficient, and in places where there are no dunes, heavy sea-walls, or dykes, have been built.

At one very vulnerable part of the coast, the force of the sea is so great that there are three dykes, one behind the other. The first is the main one, and the others are the second and third lines of defence. They are called the *Waker* (the watcher), the *Slaper* (the sleeper), and the *Dromer* (the dreamer). The 'sleeper' and the 'dreamer' rarely have to wake up, but it is very necessary that they should be there in readiness.

Dyke building

Holland is a small country. Its greatest length from north to south is about 200 miles, its greatest width 120 miles.

It would be an even smaller country if it had been left to nature. Man has won nearly half the area from the water. The *reclaimed* areas are now pumped dry, but they are still well below sea-level.

The work of draining land began in the thirteenth century, and it still goes on today. The reclaimed sections (polders) are protected by dykes. The surplus water is pumped into canals, from where it is discharged into rivers and carried to the sea. The process of reclamation is described on pages 10 and 11.

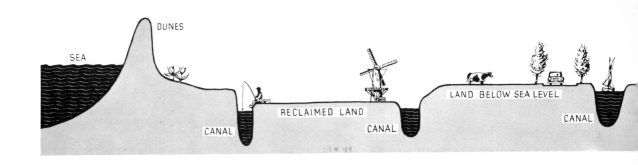

SEA   DUNES   RECLAIMED LAND   LAND BELOW SEA LEVEL   CANAL   CANAL   CANAL

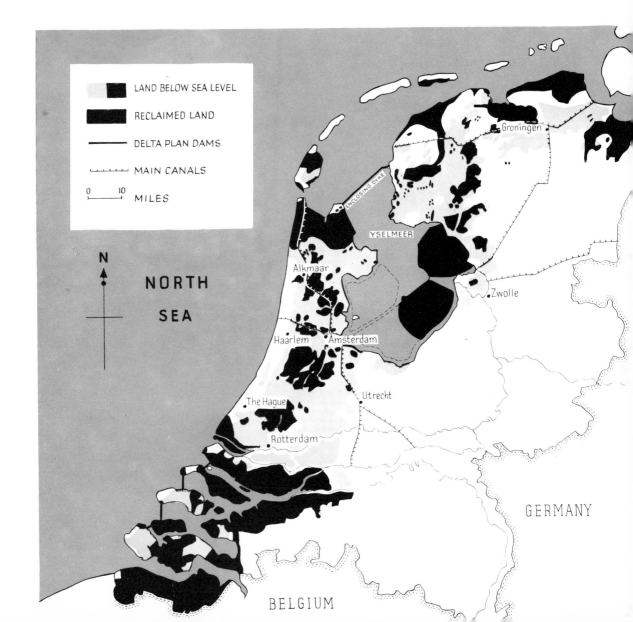

LAND BELOW SEA LEVEL

RECLAIMED LAND

DELTA PLAN DAMS

MAIN CANALS

0   10   MILES

N

NORTH SEA

Groningen

ENCLOSING DYKE

YSELMEER

Alkmaar

Zwolle

Haarlem   Amsterdam

Utrecht

The Hague

Rotterdam

GERMANY

BELGIUM

A large willow hurdle being towed into position

The photographs on these two pages show four of the stages in the making of a polder.

The average depth of the Yselmeer (Zuider Zee) is about 12 feet. An area of water along the coast is selected for drainage and from the land a dyke is built round it. This is done by making two parallel walls of heavy clay (Boulder clay) which is discharged through the bottom of a ship until it shows above the surface of the water.

The walls are strengthened by sinking on the outside large hurdles made of woven willow branches. They are weighted with stones, first heavy ones and then smaller ones. This stops the clay from being washed away.

The space between these walls is filled with sand, which makes a solid dyke about as wide as a road. The surface of the dyke is eventually strengthened and made suitable for traffic.

The completed dyke encloses a vast area of water. The next step is to pump out this water, leaving the sea-bed exposed. At first this is a soft mass, often with dangerous quicksands.

Deep trenches are then dug over the whole of the sea-bed to drain away the water still more. These are eventually replaced by pipes, which drain the land to a considerable depth and at the same time remove much of the salt. Gradually the land becomes healthy and suitable for growing normal crops. Roads are made, trees planted and villages and towns built.

The pumping was originally done by windmills, but most of them have now been replaced by modern pumping stations. Windmills are no longer as common as they used to be: only 1200 are left (there were 7000 in the seventeenth century)

In the recently reclaimed Yselmeer (Zuider Zee) polders, new villages and small towns were planned even before the land was dry. They have become prosperous communities in record time.

In Roman times the Zuider Zee was a fairly small fresh-water lake called the Flevomeer. But in the sixteenth century the North Sea broke through, bringing with it salt water.

Schemes for reclaiming the Zuider Zee started about two hundred years ago, but the technical problems were too difficult for those days. In 1920 Dr. Lely completed his plans for enclosing the Zuider Zee, and work began. This tremendous piece of engineering was finished in 1932: the sea had become a lake again; the Ysel lake or Yselmeer (see the map on page 9).

Sluices control the water level, and locks allow fishing-boats to pass through.

Dr. Lely's statue stands at the beginning of the 20-mile long enclosing dyke, which connects Noord Holland with Friesland. The dyke is nearly 100 yards wide, with a fine main road along the top.

Next, Lely's plans for more new polders were carried out: he hoped for an addition of 553,000 acres to the country's land-area. Over half of this project is now complete and work is continuing on the remainder. As each polder is reclaimed and cultivated, more experience is gained, which makes the next polder easier. The reclaimed land cannot be used for farming immediately because of the amount of salt in it. It takes from one to three years to reduce this amount of salt sufficiently, but once this is done the soil is very fertile. The up-to-date farms on the new land are in great demand, so the government can choose the most efficient and capable people to run them. This ensures that the best possible use is made of the land.

The polders provide more space for Holland's population of over 11 million to live in, and land for them to work on. A town in one of the polders has been named *Lelystad* (Lely-town) after Dr. Lely, to whom the country owes so much.

Fishing boats passing through a lock in the Yselmeer en-closing dam

Urk, once a small island, is now part of the mainland

Floods in
1953

The Zuider Zee Museum at Enk-huizen, housed in the warehouses of the old East India Company, shows interesting relics of the old Zuider Zee. During the work of drainage, wrecks and interesting archaeological finds are often discovered. Many of these can be seen in the museum on the former island of Schokland.

This and other islands such as Urk and Marken are now places on the mainland. The inhabitants, whose main occupation used to be fishing, often find it difficult to adapt themselves to the new life. Many of the young people there now work on farms and in factories instead.

In Zeeland more dyke-building is in progress, mainly for defensive purposes. The Delta plan was started in 1958. It aims to close four of the largest estuaries against the menace of storm floods. By closing the estuaries the coast-line will be made shorter, which will make the dykes easier to maintain (see the map on page 9). The Dutch hope that the new dykes will prevent disasters like the one in February 1953 when over 1500 people lost their lives. Also the existing farm land will be protected against further salting up. Two wide waterways—one leading to Rotterdam, one to Antwerp—will be left open.

A flourishing Zeeland industry, the cultivation of mussels and oysters, will disappear, but the government hope to start new industries in the province, and the fresh water lakes will attract many holiday makers.

The rest of the Dutch coastline is for the greater part protected by sand-dunes. These beautiful, well-wooded, sandy hills are a paradise for nature-lovers. Some parts, especially in the North Sea islands, have been turned into bird-sanctuaries.

Wide beaches stretch along the whole North Sea coast, from one popular resort to the next. On the beaches many people sit in wicker beach-chairs which keep out the cool winds, so that they can enjoy the sunshine in comfort.

Scheveningen

Biljoen castle in Gelderland

Before Amsterdam was linked with the North Sea, trading vessels used the Zuider Zee ports. Thus Hoorn and Enkhuizen were once important, prosperous towns. The magnificent merchant houses speak of their old glory. Although they are now dead as far as commerce is concerned, they are still mentioned in all tourists' guides, and described as "artists' paradises". There is no doubt about that—they are.

Away from the North Sea coast and the polder country, the landscape is very different. Gelderland has large wooded areas, popular as holiday resorts. Many castles and country mansions have been built here. In the south of this province, the fertile land between the rivers Rhine and Meuse is called the *Betuwe*. Most of Holland's orchards are in this area.

Noord Brabant has extensive moors. In its capital 'sHertogenbosch stands one of the finest cathedrals in the Netherlands. In Limburg the gently sloping country is much more like the landscape of Germany and Belgium than like the rest of Holland. Most Limburgers speak three languages—or a charming mixture.

The people of Friesland belong to a different race from the rest of the Netherlanders, and feel very strongly about it. The Frisian language is spoken by the majority of people in the province. Most Frisians are tall and fair. Their province has wide open spaces with stately farms, famous for their dairy-produce. The Frisian lakes are famous for yachting and skating.

The *hunebedden* (giants' beds) in Drenthe are pre-historic relics. They are some 50 groups of huge smooth boulders, probably deposited here in the Ice-age, and used by the earliest inhabitants for their tombs.

'sHertogenbosch cathedral

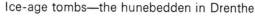

Ice-age tombs—the hunebedden in Drenthe

17

Amsterdam

About seven hundred years ago fishermen found the mouth of the River Amstel a safe shelter for their boats. They wished to settle there, but the land was very marshy, so they built a dam across the river as a foundation for their houses. This settlement was the beginning of Amsterdam, the capital of the Netherlands and one of its most beautiful cities.

Amsterdam is very proud of its canals. They were dug, from about 1600 onwards, to enlarge the busy centre, and they help to give the city a character of its own. They are lined with trees and have roads on either side. A great many bridges cross the canals, each of a different design. Barges are used for the transport of heavy goods, but there is no passenger traffic, apart from special launches carrying sightseers.

Along the canals are many noble buildings, most of them built in the seventeenth century for rich merchants to live in. Many of these stately homes have now been converted into offices, banks and consulates.

All the canals run into the IJ, Amsterdam's harbour, which used to be part of the Zuider Zee. Although not actually on the sea, the city is linked to the North Sea by a wide waterway. IJmuiden, where this North Sea Canal ends, has the largest locks in the world. So even the biggest liners can reach the IJ, and this has made Amsterdam an extremely busy port.

Amsterdam lies well below sea-level, so buildings need strong foundations. These are made by driving heavy concrete piles into the soft ground. (Originally, they were made of wood.)

The heart of the city is the old square in the centre, the Dam. In the middle of the seventeenth century an imposing new Town Hall was built there. Over thirteen thousand piles were needed for its foundations. When Napoleon's brother Louis became king of Holland, he used this building as a palace, and it has remained a royal residence ever since.

There are some very attractive shopping streets. The number of tourists going to Holland has increased considerably in the last twenty years and many new shops have opened to meet their needs. The Kalverstraat must be one of the busiest streets in the world, although only pedestrians are allowed to use it.

The modern parts of the city are well-planned and pleasant, and more and more people want to live there. But houses cannot be built quickly enough for them, so in recent years some five thousand people have made their homes in houseboats.

Traffic is a big problem in Amsterdam. Every year more and more cars and bicycles crowd the busy roadways, and the trams (trolleys) are built longer and longer to carry as many passengers as possible. Trams on routes via the Central Station are fitted with detachable letterboxes on weekdays. They are emptied when the tram stops at the station. The letters are immediately sorted in a special post office there, and are soon on their way.

Amsterdam is famous for its fine music, it has many concert halls, the best known of which is the Concertgebouw. Its resident orchestra is known all over the world.

Most churches have a set of bells and their own melody. At regular intervals throughout the day you can hear their gay, tinkling tunes.

Many office workers travel into the city every day, from their homes on the outskirts. They either cycle or come by car; the cars are often parked between the trees on the edge of a canal. Twice a week on an average the fire-brigade is called to haul out a car that has accidentally slipped into the water.

The Rijksmuseum, the National Gallery, contains valuable art treasures. This is the permanent home of Rembrandt's famous *Night Watch* and you can see paintings by all the great Dutch artists here.

In the Stedelijk Museum, the Municipal Gallery, there are more modern paintings, including many by van Gogh.

Most cafés and restaurants have pavement terraces. Passing by you can smell freshly made coffee and cigar smoke. Only one more thing is needed to complete the true atmosphere of Amsterdam: the music of a large, ornate street organ.

The Hall of Knights

The Hague

There are three large towns in the west of the country. The Hague is one of these. It is a quiet city of luxurious private houses and very few factories. The pleasant surroundings and the closeness of the sea add to its attraction.

Scheveningen is part of The Hague. It was once a small fishing-village and is now the largest seaside-resort in the country (see the photographs on page 15). Many people go there for their summer holidays. During the Holland Festival which is held every year, well known orchestras and soloists play at the famous *Kurhaus*.

Although Amsterdam is the capital of the Netherlands, Parliament meets in The Hague, in the majestic buildings of the *Binnenhof* (Inner Court). Every year on the third Tuesday in September Queen Juliana opens the two Chambers of the States-General in the *Ridderzaal* (Hall of Knights), where she makes a speech from the throne. This magnificent Hall, which forms part of the *Binnenhof*, was built in the thirteenth century.

The Peace Palace is a more recent building. In it the International Court of Justice meets. Thirty-three different countries gave contributions to its fine interior.

In the art galleries are many celebrated paintings; the most famous art gallery is the Mauritshuis.

Near The Hague a lovely 'model-town' has been built: it is called Madurodam. Here you can see all the different styles of Dutch architecture, reduced to one twenty-fifth of their actual size; Holland in a nutshell.

Madurodam

Rotterdam

Rotterdam's situation on the Meuse estuary, with direct access to the North Sea, has made it one of the gateways to western Europe. In population it is the second largest city in the country.

When Rotterdam was almost completely destroyed by bombs in 1940, it may have seemed to outsiders that its days of prosperity were over, and that this was the end. But the stubborn inhabitants would not give in. During all the long years of the war, in spite of German oppression and persecution, they made their plans for rebuilding the city and its huge artificial port.

By 1950 the port had been rebuilt and was the most up-to-date in the world, ready for international shipping once more. Rotterdam is now the leading port of Europe.

Soon the city itself was being re-built, in a style completely different from the old Rotterdam, yet still keeping the main characteristics of the city. In the shopping area there are covered walks, and shoppers can wander freely, without having to cross roads or worry about traffic.

Near the port is a striking sculpture by a Frenchman, Zadkine. It is called *The Destroyed City* and is a reminder of the horrors of war.

The tunnel under the river Meuse helps to speed the traffic between north and south, especially between Rotterdam and Antwerp.

The Market Place, Haarlem with the Church of St. Bavo,

Some Smaller Towns

Just over 10 miles separate Amsterdam from HAARLEM, home of the famous seventeenth century painter Frans Hals. The Frans Hals Museum is one of the many picturesque old buildings in the city, and around the great Market Square there are examples of most periods of Dutch architecture. Mozart and Handel both played the splendid organ in the church of St. Bavo. The surrounding country is delightful: bulb fields, woods and sand-dunes, with the sea about 5 miles away.

LEIDEN is famous for its university, which was founded to commemorate the siege of the town in the Eighty Years' War.

Then there is DELFT, where the lovely pottery is made. The canals are narrow and shady, and give the ancient little town an air of peacefulness. It was here that William the Silent spent the latter part of his life. His tomb is in the New Church, which has since become the resting-place of most of the later members of the House of Orange. Another famous Dutchman was buried here: Hugo de Groot, commonly known as 'Grotius', the founder of international law.

In the heart of the country lies UTRECHT, where in May and September the International Industries Fair is held. Utrecht's canals are unusual—they are far below street level. Under the roads are cellars belonging to the stately old houses that were once inhabited by noblemen and rich merchants.

Delft ware

For miles around, the splendid tower of the cathedral can be seen: it is the highest tower in Holland and commands a fine view of the polders and the hills beyond. The unusual thing about it is that it stands by itself. The nave collapsed in 1674, and there is still a large square between the tower and the actual cathedral.

The folk museum, Arnhem

Throughout the world the name of ARNHEM brings back memories of the Second World War. The beautiful city has now completely recovered from its devastation and attracts many visitors. Some are pilgrims who visit the war cemeteries. Others want to see the Open Air Museum. Here, set in magnificent parkland, Holland's culture through the ages is on show. There are contributions from every province, of windmills, farms, old cottages, different types of bridges etc. Costumes of the various regions can be seen, and old rural customs, bringing the past to life.

GRONINGEN has for centuries been an important centre of commerce. It is a city of great architectural beauty, and among its very fine buildings is the fifteenth century St. Martin's Church.

In all Dutch towns, large and small, the town hall is one of the most important buildings. It is often quite impressive, and beautifully designed. All towns look clean, prosperous and progressive. They have excellent shops, beautiful parks and modern swimming-pools.

The People and Their Homes

Holland is the most densely populated country in the world, so many people live in flats (apartments), especially in the towns. The flats are not usually very large. An average middle class home contains one living room, three bedrooms, a kitchen, and a very small bathroom with washbasin and shower-bath. Showers are more popular than baths and they save valuable space.

The wooden stairways leading to the several flats in one building are always carpeted. Often these stairs are so steep and narrow that furniture has to be moved through the windows. The windows are first taken out, and the furniture is then lifted up on strong ropes suspended from a big beam. (In the photograph on page 19 the beam can be seen at the top of each building.)

Dutch living rooms look cosy and warm. There is often central heating; otherwise a large, partly built-in anthracite stove is used. Under the large ceiling-light in the middle of the room stands a round or square table. This is covered with a colourful rug-like cloth, of the kind that has been used in Holland for centuries. Some families prefer more modern folk-weave material.

A modern living room

The Dutch are a very home-loving people. They like to spend their evenings sitting round the big table, reading and talking.

There are pictures and photographs on the walls, and a tremendous number of plants and flowers.

Newspapers are delivered in the evening. They are planned to be read by all the family, and most of them include a section for children.

Most Dutchmen are keen smokers, and cigars are very popular. They are cheaper than in most countries, and it is quite common to see ordinary workmen smoking cigars.

The bedrooms in Dutch homes are normally quite small. They usually have a washbasin each. To save space some people use beds that can be folded up against the wall.

The water is heated by gas or electricity; there is a special cheap rate if this is done during the night. There are no airing-cupboards in Dutch houses.

On the street doors of most houses are name plates. The most common surnames are Jansen, Smit, de Groot. Names such as van Doorn (*van* is not written with a capital V) do not indicate noble descent. They indicate the place the person came from when surnames were first used—in this case, Doorn. In Friesland many surnames end in -stra, e.g. Veenstra, Hoekstra; in Groningen the ending -ma is common, e.g. Fokkema, Douma.

On meeting a Dutchman, and murmuring a polite "How do you do"?, do not be surprised if he shakes your hand vigorously, makes a slight bow and announces "de Groot", or whatever his name may be. If his English is not very good, so that he does not recognize the "How do you do" as a casual greeting, he may even go into details about his health! It is just the Dutch way of introducing oneself. They are great handshakers on all sorts of occasions — whenever people meet, whenever they part. If they are guests in somebody's house they shake hands when bidding their host or hostess goodnight.

Below the milkman's hand is the name-plate

In Rotterdam

When two people are engaged to be married, both the man and the girl wear a plain gold ring on the left hand, and the same ring is changed over to the right hand after the wedding. The woman takes her husband's name, but she does not entirely discard her maiden name. For example, if Mr. de Groot married Miss M. Zwart, then letters to her after her marriage would be addressed *Mevrouw* (Mrs) M. de Groot-Zwart, and her name would appear like this on her visiting card. These are still in common use.

Jan, Piet and Willem are the most common boys' names; for girls Annie, and its diminutive Anneke, Marie (-ke) and Johanna (Joke) are very popular. Recently double Christian names have become popular: e.g. Jan Willem, Anne Marie. As in other countries, some children's names are taken from films and books. Refugees from other countries have always found a home in Holland, so there are many foreign names: French (Huguenots), Polish, Portuguese and German (Jews), and English (Quakers).

Just over half the population of the Netherlands is Protestant. The other half consists mainly of Catholics (39 per cent), the south of the country being almost all Catholic. There are about fifty different Protestant denominations. The various religious groups have their own schools, newspapers, broadcasting companies, trade unions, sports clubs etc.

There are very few millionaires and very few really poor people. The general standard of living is high and there is an atmosphere of prosperity both in the towns and country. The social services are excellent. The sick and disabled in particular are well cared for, and generous provision is made for the aged.

Food

Though plain and sometimes a little unimaginative, Dutch food is always palatable and good to eat. Breakfast is a simple meal: there is bread on the table (not only white and brown, but often also black ryebread); butter, wafer-like slices of cheese, and jam. Rusks and *ontbijtkoek* (breakfast cake) are popular too. Most people have tea, often without milk, with breakfast. Children drink milk, buttermilk or yogurt. They are taught to eat their *boterham* (a slice of bread and butter with cheese, jam or something else on it) with a knife and fork.

The usual eleven o'clock drink is coffee. The cafés are crowded at that time of the morning. In summer the customers sit out on the café terraces; a brightly coloured awning protects them from the heat of the sun.

Lunch is very similar to breakfast, except that there may be some ham or smoked fish, or peanut butter. This meal is called *Koffiedrinken* as most people drink coffee with it. People working in offices, teachers, schoolchildren and others who are away from home at midday take sandwiches for this meal.

The main meal is at about 6 o'clock; it is the only cooked meal of the day. It sometimes starts with very nourishing soup, then meat (often braised) or fish with plenty of potatoes and vegetables, followed by a milk pudding and fruit. Butter is liberally used in cooking.

Most people have tea in the afternoon, and either coffee or tea in the evening. In winter snackbars are busy all day serving quick cups of thick pea soup (with pieces of smoked sausage in it).

Education

The Dutch are great believers in education, and the standard is very high. Children have to go to school from the ages of six to fourteen. Parents are free to choose between the many different kinds of schools provided.

There are many private schools as well as the State schools. The private schools are very often Church schools (either Protestant, Catholic or Jewish), and religious instruction is naturally one of the subjects taught. In State schools children can have religious instruction if they wish to, after normal school hours, but there is no morning assembly and no prayers.

Most schools start at 9 a.m. and finish at 4 p.m., with a break from 12 till 2 for lunch. Wednesdays and Saturdays are half-days, but there is school on Saturday mornings.

Many children cycle to school, and if they cannot go home for lunch they bring their midday sandwiches. Meals are never provided by the school.

If a pupil is not ready for the next class at the end of a school year, he has to repeat that year's work. That is why there are always pupils of different ages in the same class—and it also explains why some slower children never get beyond the primary school. Primary schools generally have a six year course, so most children go to a secondary school at the age of twelve.

In all types of secondary school English, French and German are taught. Naturally a small country like Holland finds it vitally necessary to include foreign languages in the curriculum. It is a common experience for an English-speaking person to find that almost every Dutch person he meets can speak reasonable and sometimes fluent English. In the *Gymnasium*, the Grammar School, Latin and Greek are taught as well.

Dutch is a Germanic language. Only about fifteen million people understand it: the Dutch, Flemish-speaking Belgians and Afrikaans-speaking South Africans. Because of this the great names in Dutch literature are not generally known abroad.

Many families
live on barges

After passing their examinations Dutch children have a choice of six universities and five institutes of higher education (e.g. the Technological Institute at Delft). They are all non-residential, so all students live at home or in lodgings.

Many Dutch families live on barges, carrying goods up and down the rivers and canals. Most of the time they are on the move; they only stop for a short while for loading or unloading their cargo. Their children are educated at special schools in the principal towns they visit. For the long spells of journeying (sometimes as far as Belgium, Germany or Switzerland) they are given plenty of home-work which they hand in and discuss at the school in their next port of call.

As is usual on the continent of Europe, the Dutch use the metric system for their coins, weights and measures. The unit of currency is the *gulden* (about 2 shillings). This is divided into 4 *kwartjes*, or 10 *dubbeltjes*, or 100 *cents*.

A *kilo* is 1000 grammes; it equals 2 (Dutch) pounds or 10 (Dutch) ounces.

Dutch stamps are the joy—or despair—of philatelists. New designs are regularly issued either in commemoration of a historic event or for some national charity.

Buying a stamp

Transport

Holland has so many rivers and canals that a good deal of inland transport is by ship. Almost every part of the country can be reached that way. The ships range from the huge Rhine barges with family accommodation to the small punts which are so necessary in a place like Giethoorn. The Rhine barges are also used for international transport.

Ships on the canals often seem to sail across the fields

The mercantile marine with its coasters, tankers, cargo ships and liners carries goods and passengers all round the world. The railway system is controlled by the government and is very efficient. The trains are comfortable and always clean. Most lines are electrified or have diesel trains, so the stations are not dirty or full of smoke. Many stations had to be rebuilt after the Second World War. Station-masters take a pride in these up-to-date attractive buildings, which very often have well laid-out gardens and excellent restaurants.

On the platforms you can buy fruit, cartons of coffee and other refreshments from a trolley service.

Just outside Amsterdam is Schiphol, the country's largest airport. Sitting in the restaurant there, watching the planes landing and taking off, it is hard to realise that all the surrounding country was once a wide expanse of water. The "Ship-hole" was a particularly deep and dangerous place where many ships went down. It is still 13 metres below sea level. This is the home of the K.L.M. (Royal Dutch Airlines) well-known throughout the world as "The Flying Dutchman".

More and more bus services are being started, but there are still many trams running, especially in the large towns. Most of them have trailers. Fares are generally a fixed amount, and you can go any distance on your ticket. Within a certain time limit you can even change to another tram without having to pay again.

The bicycle track beside a modern road

Fine roads connect the main cities. Everywhere in Holland you see bicycles, and almost all roads have separate bicycle tracks. Bicycles are still the most popular form of private transport, and are ridden by rich and poor, young and old.

The flat countryside is very good for cycling. But headwinds can make pedalling very hard work, although the trees along the roadside give some shelter and help to lessen the force of the wind. Parking places for bicycles—mostly slotted paving stones—are provided everywhere in town and country alike.

Many tradesmen use outsize tricycles instead of vans for carrying their goods.

Some tradesmen use bicycles

A more modern way of delivering milk

The Philips factory

Industry

Holland is an industrial country. Forty-three percent of the population work in factories of some sort. The best-known of these are the Philips factories at Eindhoven, where electric light bulbs, radio and television sets and hundreds of other articles are made. This huge concern, which is now well established all over the world, was started in 1891 as a small father-and-son factory. Originally they only made electric light bulbs.

The shipbuilding industry is mainly in Amsterdam and Rotterdam.

Before the Second World War Amsterdam was the hub of the world's diamond industry; it now ranks second after Antwerp. Steel, food, clothing, motor-cars and many other things are all manufactured in different parts of the country.

In Delft the original pottery factory *De Porceleyne Fles* is still making its famous products. This business, which began about 1600, started by making imitations of porcelain imported from Japan. Since then the word *Delft* has come to mean blue and white pottery; the factory's speciality.

Making clogs at Best, near Eindhoven

Holland is famous for its flower industry

Another big industry is the growing of flowers and plants, especially round Aalsmeer where there is a large auction room, and a market-hall in which the flowers are displayed for sale. The auction room is partly built over a canal, and the flowers arrive in barges. Aalsmeer is very close to Schiphol Airport, from where the carefully packed flowers are flown all over the world.

The best soil for bulbs is found at the back of the sand dunes between Haarlem and Leiden. The whole area is covered with rectangular fields of daffodils, tulips and hyacinths, and in spring-time it is a glorious sight.

The shop window of the bulb industry is the *Keukenhof* at Lisse. Millions of bulbs are on show here in lovely surroundings, in sixty-five acres of woodland.

Just south of the bulb-growing area, between The Hague and the Hook of Holland, is another famous industry: the growing of vegetables, fruit and flowers in greenhouses. Enormous quantities are exported, especially grapes and tomatoes.

From olden times beef and dairy farming have been important in Holland. Edam cheese, red and ball-shaped, is still made at many farms, but more and more milk is being sent direct to cheese factories.

Keukenhof—the shop-window of the bulb industry

The cheese market at Alkmaar

This building contains the machinery which pumps brine from the large underground salt deposits

The chief market for Edam cheese is at Alkmaar. Here, every Friday morning, the cheeses are brought to the splendid old Weighhouse. They are weighed and sold, the sale being completed by the seller and the buyer shaking hands. The cheeses are then whisked off to waiting barges or lorries (trucks) by cheese-porters in traditional uniform.

Other kinds of cheese are made in Friesland, Gouda and Limburg. Leiden cheese is spiced with cumin seeds and cloves.

Leerdam, a little south of Utrecht, is justly famous for its glassware. There are ten coal-mines in the province of Limburg in the south of Holland. Salt is found in Overijsel, and oil in Drenthe. Holland is fortunate in having a rich source of natural gas ("earthgas").

Fishing is one of the oldest industries. In May, the sailing of the herring fleet is accompanied by traditional festivities. A sample of the first catch is always sent to the queen.

The herring fleet in harbour

Everywhere people enjoy this "new" herring, either in their homes or at stalls at street corners. The fish is filleted, sprinkled with finely chopped onion, and eaten raw.

Enormous numbers of eels are caught in the Yselmeer, and smoked eel, an expensive delicacy, is always in great demand. The waters of Zeeland are famous for mussels and oysters.

Eating
raw
herring

Sport and Amusements

In a country with so many lakes, rivers and canals, there are plenty of opportunities for swimming, rowing, sailing and fishing, and water-sports are very popular.

In winter, when the canals and lakes, and sometimes even the rivers and parts of the Yselmeer are frozen over, a great many people skate.

Schoolchildren always have one or two extra half-days free during the coldest weeks, so that they can enjoy this national sport. They never go out without a few small coins to give to the *baanveger* (ice-sweeper). These men keep the tracks clear of the powdery ice that is caused by much skating.

During the weekend many people go on skating-trips to other towns or villages. Occasional stops at improvised ice-cafés increase the general enjoyment and friendly atmosphere of these trips. In these booths, where the patrons slide to a sit-down on long, trestle-like seats, hot saffron-milk, cocoa and pea-soup are served to warm them, and to strengthen them for the next stage of their journey.

The Eleven Towns Race,

The greatest event is the *Eleven Towns Race*, held in Friesland when all the canals and lakes are frozen.

Football is the next most popular sport. The highlight of the year for football-fans is the Holland-Belgium match, held in the huge Olympic Stadium in Amsterdam.

Bicycles are used for pleasure as well as for work. In international cycle-races Dutch competitors usually do very well.

As they are a home-loving people the Dutch find many excuses for having celebrations and parties. Birthdays are always occasions of family gatherings.

There are innumerable presents. Before the actual day a list of suggestions is circulated among relations and friends, so that every gift is really welcome. There is coming and going all day long. It is quite a job to keep all the plates, cups and glasses continually filled. When visitors arrive or leave there are handshakes all round.

For young people their 18th birthday is especially important. It is then that they come of age. In Holland a 21st birthday has no special significance.

TOP Bicycles must use the special track
LEFT Sailing is another popular sport

48

Wedding anniversaries are great events: the first to be celebrated is the Copper wedding, after twelve and a half years of marriage.

The coming of television has done much harm to many forms of entertainment; cinemas especially have suffered. However, many American, British, French, German and Italian films (movies) are shown. The dialogue is in the foreign language, but Dutch captions are given on the screen.

Holland has its own film-industry, but the market for Dutch-speaking films is very limited, so the output is small. In the past few years, however, some very good documentaries have been made. You can book seats in advance in all cinemas.

Every town has a very active cultural life, in which people from the surrounding country-district join. Many places have their own orchestra, while theatrical and ballet companies give regular performances.

In theatres and concert halls the coffee-room plays an important part. During the long interval excellent coffee is served in these attractive rooms, which adds to the enjoyment of the evening. Ballroom dancing is very popular.

The owners of these bicycles are at a football match

Festivals

December 5th, St. Nicholas Eve, is the most popular festival of the year. St. Nicholas, one time Archbishop of Myra, was a very kind and generous person. He became the patron saint of merchant cities (such as Amsterdam), and also the patron saint of children, who affectionately call him Sinterklaas. In English-speaking countries this name has changed into Santa Claus.

The legend of St. Nicholas arriving from Spain by boat, and riding over the roof tops to drop presents down the chimneys is still kept alive. When they arrive in Amsterdam at the end of November, the Saint and his Moorish servants are officially welcomed by the Burgomaster, and ride in procession through the streets, which are lined with thousands of children.

Now a wonderfully exciting time begins. Presents are bought or made for relatives and friends, but everything has to be done secretly as all the gifts are supposed to come from Sinterklaas. The most ingenious wrappings are thought of.

St Nicholas rides in procession through Amsterdam

Children and adults alike rack their brains for amusing rhymes to go with their presents, which on the great evening seem to appear from nowhere. Everywhere the excitement is felt. Most places close early on December 5th, including most of the shops which have been competing with each other in fine window displays.

Marken children with St Nicholas

The traditional drink that evening is hot *bisschopswijn*, while *banket* (almond paste rolled in flaky pastry) and *speculaas* (spiced biscuits) are on every table.

Christmas is a much quieter festival. It is true that some people give presents again, but most people just have a family-gathering and listen to the children singing carols by the Christmas tree. Church services are always well-attended.

▲St Nicholas and Black Peter delivering presents
On the eve of St Nicholas Day ▶ children put their shoes by the chimney. Sometimes they put a carrot in for St Nicholas's horse, and when they look next morning the carrot has gone and in its place there are sweets and toys

Roast hare or roast duck are very popular as the main course of the Christmas dinner.

On December 31st large quantities of doughnuts and apple fritters are made in almost every home—not only to be eaten that evening but also to be offered to visitors the next day. New Year's Day is a general holiday, on which relations and friends are visited. The New Year is welcomed in the noisiest possible way!

The Royal Family (the House of Orange) has a warm place in the hearts of all Dutch people, whatever party or religion they belong to. The people show their loyalty especially on the queen's birthday, which is a general holiday.

Towns and villages look gay with red white and blue flags and everywhere people wear 'orange' buttonholes.

Queen Juliana receiving flowers on her birthday

Thousands make their way to Soestdyk Palace, the charming unpretentious royal residence. There the queen stands on the Palace steps and happily and graciously receives flowers and gifts from her people.

These gifts show how much the country appreciates the queen's hard work and devotion to her task.

The kermis at Amersfoort

No kermis is complete without some poffertjes

Every village and some of the towns hold an annual fair called *kermis*. However small the village may be, it is always thickly crowded at kermis-time. All the people are visited by relations and the peasantry of the surrounding country gather together to take part in the fun.

There are plenty of stalls where one may buy all sorts of cheap novelties. There are roundabouts and swings, palmists and fat ladies, and many of the modern electrical devices seen at fairs in every country. But there are also the old-fashioned booths where one can eat *poffertjes* and waffles.

The *poffertjes* look like small round fritters. They are cooked on the spot in full view of the customers and are eaten fresh and hot. They are made by the hundred in special tins placed over a fire. Little dabs of batter are put into each hollow, and as fast as the cook fills the hollows of one end of the tin, the *poffertjes* at the other end are cooked and ready to be served. They are put out on plates, in portions of twenty and covered lavishly with sugar and butter.

On October 3rd the city of Leiden has a special celebration. During the war against the Spanish (1558-1648) Leiden was besieged and the inhabitants were almost starving for five months before being relieved by the patriots. The first food given to the starving population was raw herrings, potatoes, carrots and onions.

October 3rd, the day of the relief, is celebrated with merry-making and fireworks, and again people eat raw herring and *hutspot*.

As a reward for their courage the Prince of Orange, William the Silent, offered the inhabitants of Leiden the choice between not paying taxes and the founding of a university. They chose to have a university. It was built in 1574 and is the oldest in the Netherlands.

A canal in Leiden

The Gravensteen,
a part of Leiden University.

Costume

In many country-districts and villages traditional costume is still worn, by both men and women. However, the number of people wearing these costumes is becoming smaller. Many young people leave their native town or village, and they are influenced by seeing modern dress on films and television.

The costume worn by the people of Volendam (see the frontispiece) is probably the best known outside the Netherlands, but there are many other costumes in different parts of the country. Much of the traditional costume still worn in country districts is just old-fashioned townwear, and in some cases it is worn mainly to attract tourists—and so to bring business to the district.

Huizen woman

Scheveningen: mending fishing nets

Staphorst costume

The "island" of Marken is now linked to the mainland by a strong dyke, but it still has a character of its own and a fairy tale quality. The costume is very elaborate—even the wooden shoes are ornately decorated. Boys up to the age of five dress like girls; the only difference is in the bonnets. (See page 51.)

In Zeeland, dress varies not only from one district to another, but there are also slight differences which show whether a person is a Protestant or a Catholic.

The women of Scheveningen still wear their traditional clothes, and local costume is generally worn in Staphorst.

Men in Urk wear a distinctive local dress

Women of Bunschoten and Spakenburg
often wear their traditional costume

Many men's costumes are completed by gold earrings and ornate silver belt buttons.

In many districts, such as Groningen and Friesland local costume has practically disappeared in everyday life, but it is still handed down from one generation to the next and worn on special occasions such as weddings.

Zeeland costume: coral or garnet necklaces, gold skull-caps or "ear irons", and costly lace bonnets go with many women's costumes

A traditional wedding party in Giethoorn

The marsh ground in many parts of the country makes wooden shoes a necessity. The thick wooden soles do not leak and make them warm in winter and cool in summer. They are much cheaper than ordinary boots or shoes. When people go indoors they leave their *klompen* on the doorstep. Inside the house the men and children go about in their stockinged feet; women often wear slippers.

History

The oldest settlers in the marshy river delta later known as the *Low Countries* were German and Celtic tribes. In due course they, like most other tribes in Europe, came under Roman rule. The cities of Utrecht, Nymegen and Maastricht were once Roman settlements—then called Ultratrajectem, Noviomagum and Mosaetrajectem. Under the Romans the battle against the water began, and the first dykes were built.

William the Silent

In the Middle Ages the country belonged to different European Emperors and Dukes in succession, all the time strengthening its own independence. It became a centre of learning and art, with men such as Erasmus and Pieter Brueghel.

The independence of the Netherlands was threatened when, in 1555, they became part of the great Spanish Empire, ruled by Philip II. When the Dutch rebelled against Philip's tax-policy, and against his intolerant treatment of Protestants, a Spanish army was sent to teach them a lesson. In 1558 war broke out—it was to last for eighty years.

Under the leadership of William, a young Prince of Orange, the *Republic of the United Netherlands* put up a tremendous fight. Many are the stories of courage. In 1584 the country lost its beloved leader, when William the Silent was assassinated. His name lives on in the *Wilhelmus*—the Dutch National Anthem, written by one of his friends. As founder of the *Orange* dynasty, William is known as the Father of the country. His sons carried on the war against Spain, which ended in 1648. The Republic of the United Netherlands had gained its freedom at last.

In spite of the continual struggle the country had prospered, and had developed into a great maritime power. Colonies had been founded in the East Indies, in America and in South Africa.

The first lakes were drained, and much fertile land was acquired. Science and art flourished. Rembrandt, Frans Hals and Vermeer painted their immortal works.

After the Eighty Years' War a conflict with England began. In four wars the Netherlands tried to maintain the supremacy of the sea. At the end of the seventeenth century the two rival countries were temporarily united, when William III of Orange became king of England. During the eighteenth century Holland's greatness began to decline: England was now master at sea, and France on land.

In 1795 French Revolutionary forces entered the country, and in 1806 Holland was made a satellite state of France, with Napoleon's brother Louis as king. However, the Dutch rose against their foreign oppressors, and in 1813, after Napoleon's defeat, the Netherlands became independent again.

So far the ruling Princes of Orange had always had the official title of *Stadhouder* (Governor). Now *Stadhouder* William V, who had fled to England, was recalled, and became King William I. He ruled over the Northern and Southern Netherlands. But the latter broke away in 1830 and became what we now know as Belgium.

As the population became larger, industry grew. From being a country of farmers, merchants and sailors, Holland became an industrial power.

During the First World War the Netherlands, under Queen Wilhelmina, managed to remain

Interior of a Dutch house,
by Pieter de Hooch (1629-1684)

neutral, but the Second World War brought ruthless German bombing, cruel oppression and starvation.

On May 5th 1945 the country was finally freed from German occupation. This day is now celebrated every year by a public holiday. Homage is paid to the many workers in the Resistance movement who lost their lives in the war, and all those who were killed are remembered. In spite of the vast devastation, Holland made an amazingly rapid recovery.

In 1949 the Dutch East Indies became independent and the name was changed to Indonesia. The Dutch territories in the West Indies were given more self-government.

In the Netherlands Parliament (the States-General) there are two Chambers. The members of the Second Chamber are elected by the people. Men and women have to be twenty-three years old before they can vote. They do not just vote for one candidate, but for an actual party. The people also elect the members of the Provincial States, which, in their turn, elect the First Chamber. A very important public department, *Waterstaat*, deals with the water control throughout the country. Towns and villages are officially known as *municipalities*, and their chief administrator is the *burgomaster*, who is a paid official.

In 1948 Queen Wilhelmina abdicated and was succeeded by her daughter Juliana. Queen Juliana and her husband Prince Bernhard have four daughters. The eldest daughter, crown Princess Beatrix, has a son Prince Alexander.

The Mill at Wijk,
by J. van Ruisdael
(1628-1682)

Index

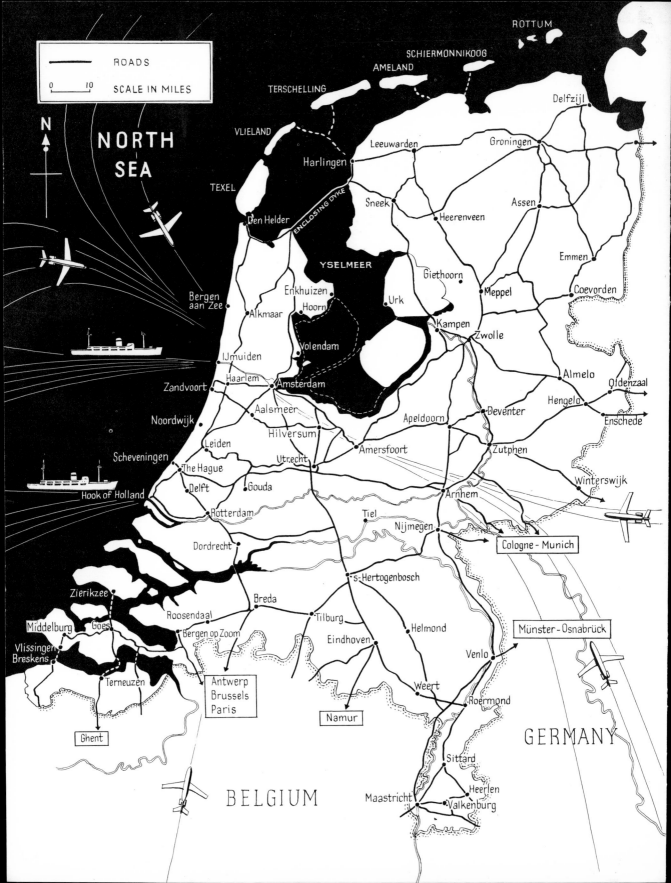